OUTLINES ON THE PARABLES OF JESUS

OUTLINES ON THE PARABLES OF JESUS

Croft M. Pentz

Baker Book House
Grand Rapids, Michigan

ISBN: 0-8010-7055-4

Thirteenth printing, January 1999

Printed in the United States of America

For information about academic books, resources for Christian
leaders, and all new releases available from Baker Book House,
visit our web site:
http://www.bakerbooks.com/

Contents

1

THE MOTE AND THE BEAM
Matthew 7:1–5

In Acts 28:3-6, we see how quick people were to judge Paul. First they said he was a murderer, later that he was a god. The Bible strongly opposes the judging of one another. Judging is a dangerous practice—it defiles and destroys. Only God is qualified to judge. He wants us to love . . . leave the judging to him!

I. Criticism and Judging—vv. 1–2
"Don't criticize, and then you won't be criticized! For others will treat you as you treat them"—LB.
A. Criticism shows a lack of Christianity—James 4:12.
B. Criticism shows a lack of control—I Cor. 9:27. God's people must learn to be Christ-controlled.
C. Criticism shows a lack of consecration. Christians are to be kind and forgiving—Eph. 4:32.

II. Concern and Judging—v. 3
Seeing the mote (small wood splinter) in a brother's eye, but not seeing the beam (log) in one's own eye:
A. Seeing another's sin: Paul told Timothy to "keep thyself pure"—I Tim. 5:22. See your own sins first; then another's shortcomings will fade. See Rom. 14:4. You are not qualified to judge others!
B. Seeing another's slackness. The Bible says that God is the judge—I Cor. 4:5. He will judge perfectly.

III. Condemnation and Judging—v. 4
"Should you say, 'Friend, let me help you get that speck out of your eye,' when you can't even see because of the board in your own"—LB.
A. Cleanse self—II Cor. 7:1. This is a daily cleansing.
B. Control self—Ps. 34:13. Keep your lips from evil. Control of the tongue often prevents trouble.
C. Consecrate self—Ps. 139:23-24. David's prayer here should be ours, also.

IV. Cleansing from Judging—v. 5

A. Personal—"Thou hypocrite." You must cleanse your own life before you can help others.

B. Purging—"First cast out the beam in thine own eye." See also I Peter 4:18.

C. Plan—"And then shalt thou see clearly to cast out the mote out of thy brother's eye." Note James 4:8. Before we can help others, we must be right with God. One cannot live hypocritically and be able to help others spiritually.

Often those who judge others' misconduct are guilty of the same sin, and criticizing another is an attempt to cover their own wrongdoing. Those who judge others are not living close to God, nor are they living successful Christian lives. Remember: we are to love people—let God judge them!

2

THE GOOD SHEPHERD
John 10:1-8

The prophet says, "All we like sheep have gone astray" Isa. 53:6. In this parable, man is compared to sheep and Christ is the Shepherd. Men are like sheep—lost in sin and in need of guidance. Christ came into the world to teach men the way to heaven; by His teaching and example, He will lead us.

I. The Comparison—vv. 1-6

A. Salvation—v. 1. Christ uses this to illustrate the way to heaven (see John 14:6, Acts 4:12).

B. Shepherd—v. 2. Christ is the great Shepherd.

C. Saviour—v. 3. The door to God's salvation is opened by Christ to those who accept His leading.

D. Strangers—vv. 4, 5. Sinners do not follow Christ because they do not know His voice.

E. Spiritual—v. 6. This parable is a spiritual lesson not understood by worldly people.

II. The Christ—vv. 7-15

A. Person—v. 7. Christ is the door. He is the only way of salvation.

8

Note the wrong way—Prov. 14:12. Christ is personal—eight times in John, He says, "I am."
B. Problem—v. 8. All those before Christ were the thieves and robbers, blinded spiritually and without understanding. They were dead in sin; He came to quicken us—Eph. 2:1.
C. Pardon—v. 9. Those who come to Christ will be saved. He turns none away (see Rom. 10:13; John 6:37). His blood cleanses us from all sin—I John 1:7.
D. Personality—vv. 10-11
  1. Life—v. 10. He came to give enjoyable life (cf. Ps. 16:11).
  2. Love—v. 11. Christ the Good Shepherd gives His life for His sheep (cf. John 15:13).
E. Practice—vv. 12-14. The "hireling" is someone to whom doing God's work is a job—not a divine calling.
F. Protection—v. 15. He gave His life for the sheep. We are always safe in Him (cf. Ps. 91).

III. **The Concern—vv. 16-18**
A. Soul winning—v. 16. The world needs Christ. Christians should not be content with their own salvation—they should feel compelled to reach the lost (Mark 16:15).
B. Surrender—v. 17. Christ gave His life willingly. He died for all people everywhere—John 3:16.
C. Sacrifice—v. 18. "No one can kill me without my consent—I lay down my life voluntarily. For I have the right and power to lay it down when I want to and also the right and power to take it again. For the Father has given me this right"—LB.

When sheep refuse to follow the shepherd, they go astray; they face the possibility of being killed by other animals. As long as we remain in Christ, and He in us, no harm can come to us. If we stray from Him, we forfeit His protection and guidance; let's follow our Shepherd closely.

3

THE WISE AND FOOLISH VIRGINS
Matthew 25:1-13

This parable stresses the importance of being ready for the coming of

Christ. He will come again—John 14:1-6. All the prophecies in Matt. 24 concerning His coming are in the process of being fulfilled. He wants His people to be awake and alert. Satan seeks to put God's people to sleep spiritually, so they will not be ready.

I. **The People—vv. 1-5**
   A. The story—v. 1. A parable to teach us readiness.
   B. The symbols—vv. 2-4
      1. The foolish. They took no extra oil, thinking that they had plenty (cf. Rev. 3:17).
      2. The wise. They were prepared with an extra supply of oil. They did not depend upon past resources.
   C. The sleeping—v. 5. While waiting for the wedding, they all slept. The wise went to sleep prepared, the foolish, unprepared (cf. Prov. 27:1).

II. **The Plan—vv. 6-9**
   A. Preparation—vv. 6-7. "The bridegroom cometh; go ye out to meet him." They trimmed their lamps. We, as Christians, must trim our spiritual lives in readiness for His coming—Matt. 24:44.
   B. Pleading—v. 8. The foolish asked the wise to give them some of their oil. They were dependent on others for entrance to the wedding feast. Each person must have a personal relationship with Jesus Christ.
   C. Personal—v. 9. The wise told the foolish to go and buy oil for themselves. No one can accept Christ for you. Each person must be born again—John 3:1-8.

III. **The Problem—vv. 10-12**
   A. Problem—v. 10. Note: "The door was shut." God gave the people in Noah's day time to prepare—Gen. 6:3.   Some day the door will be closed (see Prov. 29:1; Isa. 55:6).
   B. Plea—v. 11. "Open to us." The wise could not open the door. Only Christ can open the door—John 14:6.
   C. Punishment—v. 12. Note: "I know you not." Only those who are born again will gain entrance—John 3:1-8; Mark 16:16.

IV. **The Preparation—v. 13**
   Prepare by watching!
   A. Watch your character—I Cor. 7:1. You are developing good or bad habits. It takes a lifetime to build good Christian character.
   B. Watch your consecration—Rom. 12:1, 2. Caleb, though 85 years

old, could say that he had fully followed the Lord—Deut. 1:36. God wants full surrender, full dedication.
C. Watch your companions—II Cor. 6:17. You are known by your associations. Choose Christian friends—Amos 3:3.

Are you awake? Do you have enough oil? The oil is a symbol of the Holy Spirit. Paul tell us to be filled with the Spirit—Eph. 5:18. Don't depend on past experiences or blessings. Each day, renew the touch of God upon your life. Learn to walk in the Spirit . . . pray in the Spirit . . . live in the Spirit. As the Holy Spirit controls your life, you will be ready when the bridegroom comes.

4

THE TRUE VINE
John 15:1–17

The new birth is not the end. It is the beginning of new life in Christ, abiding in Him and He in us. As we abide in Christ, we will have His presence and power. We will produce fruit in a two-fold way: (1) Growing and maturing in Christ, and (2) winning others to Christ.

I. The Caretaker—vv. 1–2
A. The Father's care—v. 1. Christ is the vine, and His Father is the husbandman, or caretaker.
B. The Father's concern—v. 2. Our caretaker takes away that which may hinder spiritual growth (Prov. 3:11, 12).

II. The Cleanliness—v. 3
A. Cleansing the actions—Gal. 5:16. Walk in the Spirit.
B. Cleansing the attitudes—Prov. 23:7. Your attitudes not only control you, but they show your character.
C. Cleansing the affections—I Cor. 13. This love should grow daily in the life of the Christian.

III. The Cooperation—vv. 4–6
A. Detained—v. 4. Abiding in Him means fellowship—I John 1:7. Wait before Him—Isa. 40:31.
B. Dependence—v. 5. Without Him, we can do nothing—with Him, we can do all things—Phil. 4:19.

C. Destruction—v. 6. Those who don't produce fruit are cast into the fire. Jesus warns of repentance—Luke 13:3. A changed life is necessary. See II Cor. 5:17.

IV. The Consecration—vv. 7–8
  A. Prayer—v. 7
    1. Promise: abiding in Him (I John 3:6).
    2. Power: asking and receiving God's answer—Jer. 33:3.
  B. Pleasure—v. 8. The Father is glorified when we produce fruit. In so doing, we are Jesus' disciples.

V. The Commandments—vv. 9–12
  A. Steadfast love—v. 9. We should imitate God's love toward us in our relationships with others.
  B. Sure love—v. 10. If we keep His commands, we are in His love (cf. John 14:15).
  C. Successful love—v. 11. Obedience brings joy (John 16:24).
  D. Surrendered love—v. 12. Love as He loved (Matt. 22:39).

VI. The Commission—vv. 13–17
  A. Measureless love—v. 13. His love was manifested by His death upon the cross (John 3:16; I John 3:16).
  B. Method of love—v. 14. We are friends of Christ if we follow His commands.
  C. Manner of love—vv. 15–17. Love gives. Love shares. Love wins the lost. Love caused the followers of Jesus to obey—Mark 16:16–20. Because they obeyed, they had results.

Are you abiding in Christ? Do you walk and talk with Him daily? Are you growing daily—producing fruit—and reaching out to the lost for Christ? If you don't grow, you will fall by the wayside. Allow Him to abide in you. Allow Him to remove those things from your life that keep you from being the best for Him.

5

THE GOOD SAMARITAN
Luke 10:25–37

Christians must be willing to help those in need. Though salvation is not by good works (Eph. 2:8 ,9), salvation will produce good works. Some are so busy with self and pleasure that they have no time to help others; too many are interested in *getting but not giving*. If you want to enjoy the Christian life, then learn to give. Learn to share. Learn to help.

I. The Seeker—vv. 25–29
A. Desire—v. 25. A man came to Christ, seeking the way to inherit eternal life. Many sincere people are seeking for truth.
B. Demand—vv. 26–27. Note the demand made by Jesus:
1. Love God with all thy heart—our emotions.
2. Love God with all thy soul—our spiritual being.
3. Love God with all thy strength—our physical being.
4. Love God with all thy mind—our mental life.
C. Destiny—v. 28. By keeping this command, we are really fulfilling all the Ten Commandments—Exod. 20:1–16. If you love God in the four-fold way above, you will keep these commands.

II. The Story—vv. 30–35
A. Problem—v. 30. A traveler was robbed, wounded, and left along the roadside to die, alone and in need of help.
B. People—vv. 31–35. Notice the people who came by:
1. A Jewish Priest. He represents the religious world. He offered no help.
2. A Levite. He represents the church world. He also passed without helping. Those who know God will get involved and help those in need.
3. A Samaritan. He represents the Christian world. Though the Samaritans and Jews were enemies, this Samaritan helped this Jew in need.
C. Pity—The despised Samaritan had pity for the Jewish man who had been ignored by his religious leaders.
1. Divine love. He had compassion on him.
2. Practical love. He bound up his wounds.
3. Kind love. He took him to an inn and gave him shelter.
4. Unselfish love. He paid for his care.

III. The Simplicity—vv. 36–37
A. Application—v. 36. Who is your neighbor? The wounded one. The whole world is wounded—let's help them.
B. Answer—v. 37. Note Jesus' words, "Go and do thou likewise." Don't just talk about love—show it! "But if someone who is supposed to be a Christian has money enough to live well, and

13

sees his brother in need, and won't help him—how can God's love be within him?''—I John 3:17, LB.

Are you like the Good Samaritan? Do you give of your time, self, and money to help those in need? God wants more than words—He wants action. Note these steps:

a) Be considerate. Think of others, their needs and problems.
b) Be consecrated. When you give yourself to God, you will be helpful.
c) Be compassionate. Put yourself in the place of others.
d) Be Christlike. Have His love and compassion.

6

THE GREAT SUPPER
Luke 14:16–24

Jesus used this parable to explain the invitation to salvation. The Bible gives many invitations. God has done His part by giving His Son. Christ has done His part by dying on the cross. The Holy Spirit has done His part by convicting us of our sins. Despite many invitations, man continues to reject this great gift. The word for excuse has several meanings: reject, refuse, beg off, and avoid.

I. The Celebration—vv. 16–17
    A. Invitations sent—v. 16. The invitations were sent in advance. Each person had enough time to prepare for the supper.
    B. Invitations sought—v. 17. It was a custom to follow up the written invitation with a personal visit. Note some of the invitations for man today:
        1. Invitation to salvation—Matt. 11:28–31.
        2. Invitation to serve—Mark 16:15.
        3. Invitation to surrender—Rom. 12:1–2.
        4. Invitation to sacrifice—Luke 9:23.
        5. Invitation to support—Rom. 10:14–15.

II. The Complaints—vv. 18–20
Note the excuses made for not attending the supper:
    A. Purchasing excuse—v. 18. The man bought ground and wanted to

see it. No one buys ground without first seeing it. This was a very poor excuse.

B. Proving excuse—v. 19. A man bought oxen and wanted to test or prove them. No one works animals at night. Again, a foolish excuse.

C. Pleasure excuse—v. 20. Because a man had married, he could not attend. Surely his marriage did not keep him from other events.

Excuses are not acceptable to God—He knows the reason behind the excuse.

III. **The Concern—vv. 21–24**

A. Instruction—v. 21. "The servant returned and reported to his master what they had said. His master was angry and told him to go quickly into the streets and alleys of the city and to invite the beggars, crippled, lame and blind"—LB.

B. Incomplete—v. 22. There was still more room. Regardless of how many we may win to Christ, there is always room for more. We should never be satisfied. Remember Mark 16:15.

C. Invitation—vv. 23–24.

    1. Go. Go out and invite all to come—to every place—to all classes of people. (See Rom. 10:13, II Peter 3:9).

    2. Goal. Note: "That my house may be filled." God wants His church filled.

Do you make excuses? (a) For not reading the Bible? (b) For not praying? (c) For not attending church? (d) For not giving your money? (e) For not fully surrendering? (f) For not winning souls? Remember, God knows the real reasons—excuses are lies. Never make excuses, but resolve, "I will always do my best to be faithful to God." This will please God and help you to become a strong Christian.

7

THE RICH MAN AND LAZARUS
Luke 16:19–31

We have a choice—whether we will have God's heavenly reward or the fiery destruction of the wicked after death. Note these passages: (1) Psalm 9:17—those who forget God. (2) Daniel 12:2—everlasting punishment. (3)

Rev. 21:8—those doomed to the lake of fire. (4) Rev. 14:11; 20:10—no rest in hell.

I. The People in the Story—vv. 19–21
A. Man of wealth—v. 19. "There was a certain rich man," Jesus said, "who was splendidly clothed and lived each day in mirth and luxury"—LB. Some have named the rich man "Dives," the Latin word meaning rich.
B. Man of want—v. 20. The poor man begged for crumbs from the rich man's table. He had no money for medicine; the dogs came and licked his sores.

II. The Particulars in the Story—vv. 22–26
A. Heaven—vv. 22. "Finally the beggar died and was carried by the angels to be with Abraham in the place of the righteous dead. The rich man died and was buried"—LB. All will die—Heb. 9:27.
B. Hell—v. 23. "And his soul went to hell. There, in torment, he saw Lazarus in the far distance with Abraham"—LB.
C. Help—v. 24. The rich man cried out for water to cool his tongue from the heat of hell-fire. (See Mark 9:44).
D. Helpless—v. 25. It was too late to change after death. There will be no second chance, no further opportunity to repent and be converted.
E. Horror—v. 26. Once a person enters hell, he will remain. Seek Christ today—Mark 16:16.

III. The Prayer in the Story—vv. 27–31
A. Pain—vv. 27–28. The pain was great. The rich man wanted someone to warn his brothers not to go to this awful place (cf. Rev. 20:10; 14:11).
B. Prophets—v. 29. "But Abraham said, 'The Scriptures have warned them again and again. Your brothers can read them any time they want to' "—LB.
C. Proposal—v. 30. The rich man thought that if someone rose from the dead, his brothers would believe. But when Christ arose from the dead, they didn't believe it.
D. Problem—v. 31. If the rich man's brothers didn't believe Moses, neither would they believe anyone else, even if that person rose from the dead.

There is a hell. But, also, there is a heaven. Note: (1) The words of Jesus—John 14:1–3. (2) A home not made with human hands—II Cor. 5:1. (3) Abraham looked for a city made by God—Heb. 11:10. (4) Paul tells of being with Christ after death—II Cor. 5:8. (5) The Bible tells of a new heaven—Rev. 22:1-7. You can choose to accept or reject God's plan of salvation. God sends no one to hell—they send themselves by refusing to accept God's pardon.

8

THE SHEEP AND THE GOATS
Matthew 25:31-46

Many people do not think of the Christian judgment they must face. This judgment (II Cor. 5:10) is different than the judgment for sinners in Rev. 20:11-15. A Christian will be judged for his: (1) time—Ps. 90:12, (2) talent—Matt. 25:14-30, (3) tongue—Matt. 12:36, (4) thoughts—Prov. 23:7, (5) testimony—Eccles. 12:14, (6) traits—I Cor. 3:8, and (7) tithes—Mal. 3:8-10.

I. **The Saviour—vv. 21-33**
   A. The Son—v. 31. "The Son of Man" means Jesus in human form. Note these words, "The Word was made flesh"—John 1:14. Jesus became a man to understand man.
   B. The separation—vv. 32-33. There are just two classes of people—the Christian and the sinner. Christ makes the difference—I John 3:2. Note those who will be in hell—Rev. 21:8.
   Note the end-time events: Christ may return at any time. This is the *rapture*. Christians will be taken to heaven. Sinners will be on earth for seven years—this is the *tribulation*. Christians will be receiving rewards in heaven during this time. Then there will be the *millennial reign* (1,000 years) of Christ, followed by the *last judgment*—Rev. 20:11-15; and finally, the *new heaven and new earth*.

II. **The Sharing—vv. 34-40**
   A. Rewards—v. 34. Inherit the kingdom. This means we will share in the glories of heaven. All God's riches will be ours!
   B. Reason for rewards—vv. 35-36.
      1. Christian care—vv. 35-36. Christians will help (I John 3:17; James 1:27).
      2. Christian concern—vv. 37-39. The people were concerned. What did Jesus mean?

17

3. Christlike compassion—v. 40. Doing good to the least (the most unimportant person), regardless of status, was Jesus' way.

Whatever we do, we should do for the glory of God. Doing good works for the praise of man will mean forfeiting the heavenly reward.

III. The Suffering—vv. 41–46
A. Separation—v. 41. Hell is not for Christians, but for the devil and his followers.
B. Sorrow—vv. 42–43. They had no time for Christ or to help others. Good works do not produce salvation, but salvation will produce good works.
C. Sin—vv. 44–45. Know what is right, then do it (James 4:17).
D. Sentence—v. 46. Note the two-fold sentence: (1) Those who refuse to accept Christ, and (2) those who are righteous. Christ's sentence will be final.

Some Christians feel they should do just enough to get by. Some of these will find they didn't do enough to get by! Being a Christian and living the Christian life is not a job or duty—it is a privilege. Always do more than is required of you.

9
WISE AND FOOLISH BUILDERS
Matthew 7:24–29

In this parable, Jesus emphasizes two things: (1) hearing and (2) doing. Men hear, but few obey His commands. Knowing what is right is one thing—doing is quite another. Many know the Bible, but few practice it. In this passage, Jesus uses two words—wise and foolish. The measure of success and failure in the eyes of God is quite different than that of man.

I. The Wise Man—vv. 24–25
A. The symbol—v. 24. Note the application here of hearing and doing the sayings of Christ.
   1. Keep Christ's commands—John 14:15. Love for Him is judged by our obedience.
   2. Keep Christ's words—John 14:23. Love will honor Him.
B. The stability—v. 25. The winds and the storms came, but the

house remained firm because it was established upon a rock. We are kept by God's power—I Peter 1:5; I Tim. 1:12; Jude 24.

II. The Foolish Man—vv. 26–27

A. The disrespect—v. 26. When disobeying Jesus' commands, we are like the man who built his house on the sand. There was no sure foundation.

1. Sin—James 4:17. When one knows what is right and refuses to do so, he is sinning.
2. Stubbornness—Prov. 14:12. Refusing the right way leads to death. See John 14:6.

B. The destruction—v. 27. When the storms came, the house fell. This man was unstable. Note how many heard Jesus, but turned back and refused to follow Him—John 6:66. See also:

1. II Tim. 4:10. Demas deserted Christ.
2. Rev. 20:11–15. Because of rejecting Christ, many will be condemned.

III. The Wise Message—vv. 28–29

A. The teacher—v. 28. Jesus was a teacher sent from God. The people were amazed at His doctrine. Nicodemus knew He was from God—John 3:2. Though He was divine, Jesus was also human. He wept—John 11:35.

B. The teaching—v. 29. What did He teach? His teaching met all the needs of mankind, spiritual and material.

How are you building? Are you obeying the teachings of Christ? David not only heard God's Word—he hid it in his heart—Ps. 119:11. Because of this, he was cleansed from sin—Ps. 119:9. Paul spoke of believing in the heart—Rom. 10:9–10. When one believes in the heart, he will put his beliefs into practice. As we practice the teachings of Christ, we are building upon a strong foundation, one that will endure eternally—I John 2:17.

10

THE PRODIGAL SON
Luke 15:11–32

In this parable, Jesus emphasized the importance of a lost soul returning to the heavenly Father. He dealt with several important areas: (1)

Rebellion—the young son rebelling against the father. (2) Riotous living of the son—living in sin never satisfies. (3) Repentance—the son saw his mistake and repented. (4) Restoration—the father restored the runaway son. (5) Rejection—the son who stayed home became angry at the love shown by the father to the prodigal son.

I. The Selfish Son—vv. 11–12

   A. Sons—v. 11. The father has two sons.

   B. Selfishness—v. 12. The younger son wanted his share of the inheritance.

II. The Sinful Son—vv. 13–14

   A. Wasting—v. 13. "A few days later this younger son packed all his belongings and took a trip to a distant land, and there wasted all his money on parties and prostitutes"—LB.

   B. Want—v. 14. "About the time his money was gone a great famine swept over the land, and he began to starve"—LB. Sow in sin, and you will reap in sorrow—Gal. 6:7-8.

III. The Sorrowing Son—vv. 15–16

   A. Humility—v. 15. The rich son became poor, and worked for a farmer, feeding pigs. See II Peter 2:22.

   B. Hunger—v. 16. He was hungry—". . . and no man gave unto him." With his money gone, his friends were gone! The ungodly friends did not come to his rescue in time of need.

IV. The Sensible Son—vv. 17–19

   A. Remembering—v. 17. The son "came to himself." In other words, "He came to his senses." He was hungry; while at home his father had plenty. God meets all our needs—Phil. 4:19.

   B. Resolution—v. 18. He decided to leave the pig pen and return home. Follow God, and He will care for you—Ps. 37:25.

   C. Resignation—v. 19. The son would say to his father, "And am no longer worthy of being called your son. Please take me on as a hired man"—LB.

V. The Sympathy Shown—vv. 20–24

   A. Compassion—v. 20. The father ran to meet him. Christ invites us to come—Rev. 3:20; Isa. 1:18.

   B. Confession—v. 21. The son confessed his mistakes. We, too, must confess to God—I John 1:9; Rom. 10:9-10.

   C. Concern—vv. 22-24. Note the father's love. God forgives and forgets—Ps. 103:3, 12.

VI. The Stubborn Son—vv. 25-32

A. Rejoicing—v. 25. The lost son has come home.

B. Request—v. 26. The older son asked the reason for the celebration.

C. Report—v. 27. Simply stated, the lost son has come home.

D. Rebellion—vv. 28-32. The older son became bitter and jealous. The father lovingly explained the joy of reinstating a lost son. Bitterness is sin.

Rejoice when a sinner repents. Regardless of a person's past life, God has forgiven and forgotten his sin. There is rejoicing in heaven when a sinner repents—Luke 15:10. If a person wastes his life, don't be critical. Show God's love and compassion toward him.

11

THE SEATS AT THE WEDDING
Luke 14:8-11

The number one enemy of the Christian is self! Satan uses self to destroy the Christian through: (1) ambitions and desires which oppose God's will, (2) attitudes which control our lives, (3) affections for "things" (I John 2:15-17). If Christ is our Lord and master, self will not be in control. We cannot serve two masters—Matt. 6:24.

I. Selfishness—v. 8

A. Seeking—v. 8a. Don't seek the best for selfish reasons. Paul said, "Not I, but Christ . . ."—Gal. 2:20.

B. Sharing—v. 8b. Shame of displacement may come to him who seeks to take highest honors for himself. Paul was a great man, but he said he was the chief of sinners—I Tim. 1:15. Paul practiced humility.

II. Shame—v. 9

A. Reservation—v. 9a. "The host will bring him over to where you are sitting and say, 'Let this man sit here instead' "—LB. Learn to live the crucified life—Gal. 2:20.

B. Result—v. 9b, "And you, embarrassed, will have to take what-

ever seat is left at the foot of the table''—LB.
Spell JOY . . . J—Jesus O—Others Y—Yourself.

III. **Sincerity—v. 10**
   A. Humble acceptance—v. 10a. Accept the low, unimportant place.
      1. Practice—James 4:10. Humble yourself. This involves deny-
         ing self—Luke 9:23.
      2. Personality—I Peter 5:5. (a) Submit to the elder (b) Be clothed
         with humility. (c) God resists the proud.
   B. Humble advancement—v. 10b.
      1. Promise—I Peter 5:5b. He gives grace to the humble.
      2. Position—James 4:10b. If we humble ourselves, He will lift us
         up.

IV. **Spirituality—v. 11**
   A. Self-honor—v. 11a, "For everyone who tries to honor himself
      shall be humbled"—LB.
      1. Satan's pride—Isa. 14:13. Satan wanted to be above God and
         was cast out of heaven.
      2. Selfish pride—Mark 10:35–37. James and John wanted to sit
         on the right hand of Christ in heaven.
   B. Spiritual honor—v. 11b, "And he who humbles himself shall be
      honored"—LB. Be faithful in small things—Luke 19:17. Then
      you will receive greater responsibilities. (See also Ps. 91:14).

When Christ is first in your life, you will not seek honor or fame—you
will seek to please Him. As you do this, you will remain humble before
Him. Humility will be rewarded both in this life and in eternity.

12

MARRIAGE OF KING'S SON
Matthew 22:1–14

Wedding feasts in the Bible were important, sometimes lasting for days.
Jesus used the wedding feast as an example of the marriage supper of the
Lamb. How often other things are deemed more important than doing the
will of God.

I. The Invitations Sent—vv. 1-7

A. The parable—vv. 1-3. Many are invited to serve Christ, but few follow. (See Matt. 7:13-14; John 6:66.)

B. The preparation—v. 4. A large meal was planned. Christ has planned a heavenly home for us—John 14:1-3. Some will accept and others reject—Mark 16:16.

C. The problem—vv. 5-6. Invitations were sent, and many rejected them. Note the rejection of Christ—John 1:11-12.

D. The punishment—v. 7. Those who rejected the invitation were destroyed. Compare the fate of those who reject Christ (Rev. 20:11-15, Rev. 21:8).

II. The Invitations Shunned—vv. 8-10

A. Corrupt—v. 8. Those invited were not worthy to attend. None are worthy of salvation. All have sinned—Rom. 3:23. We deserve to die for our sins—Rom. 6:23. We don't want justice—we need mercy.

B. Command—v. 9. Compel people to come. The word *compel* means not to quit trying. See John 15:16; Mark 16:15. Note the judgment upon those who refuse to win the lost—Ezek. 3:18.

C. Complete—v. 10. Both good and bad people attend. God wants all men to be saved—John 3:16. He doesn't want any to be lost— II Peter 3:9. He accepts all those who truly repent—Rom. 10:13; John 6:37.

III. The Indifference Shown—vv. 11-14

A. Sin—v. 11. A man was present without a wedding garment. We need the robe of Christ's righteousness. Our righteousness is as filthy rags in the sight of God—Isa. 64:6. Christ is the only way to the Father—John 14:6.

B. Speechless—v. 12. He had no excuse. When man stands before God, excuses will not be accepted—Rom. 2:1. Jesus paid the price for our salvation; to reject Him is to be lost.

C. Sorrow—v. 13. Note those who will have part in the lake of fire—Rev. 21:8.

D. Selection—v. 14. Only those who have accepted Christ will be saved. Note John 3:16—"everlasting life" to those who believe in Him.

Beware of being so busy that you have no time for God. The judgment day is coming—Rev. 20:11-15. Those who accept Christ will not face this judgment—John 5:24. Death is coming—Heb. 9:27; after this comes judgment. Heeding these verses will help you put Christ first in your life: Matt. 6:33; Matt. 22:37; Rom. 12:1–2; Prov. 3:5–6.

13

THE TALENTS
Matthew 25:14–30

God will judge man according to his use of his talents. The word *talent* means abilities, skills, intelligence, or gifts. All people have talents; some have more than others. God will judge our faithfulness in using these talents. Not all can teach Sunday school or sing in the choir. Some can clean the church; others can visit, etc. All can pray and witness for the Lord. The Bible warns us to be faithful—Rev. 2:10. Whatever you do, do it with faithfulness to God.

I. The Parable—vv. 14–18
   A. Servant—v. 14. The servants met with the master before he went on a journey. They were given money for investment purposes.
   B. Sharing—v. 15. The Living Bible says the shares were $5,000, $2,000, and $1,000. Others were given according to their ability.
   C. Service—vv. 16–17. Some put their money into service by investing it to gain interest.
   D. Shame—v. 18. The man given $1,000 hid it. Faithless and fearful, he allowed his talent to lie dormant.

II. The People—vv. 19–25
   A. The return—v. 19. After a long time, the master returned and asked an accounting of the money. We are accountable to God for our lives—II Cor. 5:10.
   B. The results—vv. 20–23. Those who invested their money were praised for their faithfulness. We, too, will be judged by our faithfulness—I Cor. 4:2.
   C. Rejection—vv. 24–26. God expects us to use the talents he gives for His honor and glory.
   D. God will judge Christians in their use of:
      1. Time—Ps. 90:12.
      2. Money—Mal. 3:8–10.
      3. Abilities and skills. See Eccles. 9:10.

III. The Punishment—vv. 26–30

A. Laziness—v. 26. "But his master replied, 'Wicked man! Lazy slave! Since you knew I would demand your profit...' "—LB. See also Rom. 12:11.

B. Loss—vv. 27–30. The talent was taken from the one who had wasted it and given to the one who had made the greatest increase. The unprofitable servant was cast into outer darkness.

C. Lesson—God's judgment will come to all people. See Heb. 9:27; II Cor. 5:10; Rev. 20:11–15.

At the judgment for Christians, there will be tears because the Christian was guilty of laziness and indifference. God's people know their need for Bible reading and prayer, they know it is right to give God His tithe, they know soul-winning is their responsibility—but so many Christians do not apply this knowledge to their lives. As the result, they will stand in shame at this judgment for Christians.

14

THE FRIEND AT MIDNIGHT
Luke 11:5–8

All people have needs. God desires to meet these needs, and often meets them through His people. In this parable we see a man with a need who would not give up or accept defeat. If you are praying according to God's Word (I John 5:14), then keep praying. Don't give up—the answer will come; perhaps not in the way you expect, but according to God's will.

I. Seeing the Need—vv. 5–6

A. Present need—v. 5. Food was needed for visitors. God wants to meet our needs—Phil. 4:19.

B. Pressing need—v. 6. Note, "I have nothing." As Christians, we show our love by helping those in need.
1. Showing our love—I John 3:17. Love always gives.
2. Sharing our love—Luke 6:38. As we give to others, God will give to us in return.
3. Spiritual love—Prov. 25:21. Feeding our enemy.
4. Surrendered love—Luke 10:34. Like the good Samaritan, help those in need.

All around us are the needy, depending upon us for help. Will you help them?

II. Selfishness and the Need—v. 7
The friend didn't want to get involved.
A. Selfish attitude. In the story of the good Samaritan, the priest and the Levite had no time to help. Surely God was not first in their lives—Matt. 6:33.
B. Selfish ambition—Luke 12:16–20. The rich farmer was preparing for himself, with no thought for others. God called him a fool.
C. Selfish affection—Matt. 22:37. When we love God, it is easy to love others—Matt. 22:39.

III. Sharing the Need—v. 8
Persistence will help us meet the need.
A. Daily prayer—James 5:16. Note the importance. David prayed three times daily—Ps. 55:17. Daily prayer means daily power and daily persistence.
B. Determined prayer—James 5:17–18. "He prayed again." He didn't quit when the answer didn't come—he kept praying.
C. Dedicated prayer—John 15:7. If we live according to God's Word, He will answer. (Cf. Ps. 37:4–5.)

True Christians will not only see the needs of others—they will supply. Love toward the Lord, as well as others, is more than mere words. The man at the door would not give up. His persistence brought results. God will answer our prayers as we persistently seek Him.

15

THE UNMERCIFUL SERVANT
Matthew 18:23–35

In God's great mercy, He gave His Son to die in our stead. Because we were born in sin (Rom. 3:23), we should die for our sins (Rom. 6:23). "But the gift of God is eternal life." It is God's desire that all repent—II Peter 3:9. When we accept God's mercy, we must show mercy toward others.

I. The Picture—vv. 23–27

A. Parable—v. 23. God's kingdom is narrowed down to the relationship between master and servant.

B. Problem—v. 24. A man owed 10,000 talents ($10,000,000—LB).

C. Punishment—v. 25. He was unable to pay the debt, and he and his family were to be sold as slaves. Jesus spoke of being slaves to sin—John 8:34.

D. Plea—v. 26. The debtor asked for mercy. Christians are to be patient and forgiving—Eph. 4:32.

E. Pardon—v. 27. The master forgave the debtor his huge debt. God forgives us from all sin—Ps. 103:3. See also I John 1:7, 9.

II. The Problem—vv. 28–30

A. Person—v. 28. The forgiven servant accosted a man who owed him $2,000. He was impatient, forgetting the tremendous debt that had been forgiven.

B. Plea—v. 29. The debtor pleaded for time to pay his debt.

C. Problem—v. 30. No patience is shown. He easily forgot the forgiveness he had received. The Bible warns us not to forget all the benefits of God—Ps. 103:2.

God forgives and forgets our transgressions. As followers of Christ, we too should forgive and forget.

III. The Principles—vv. 31–35

A. Sorrow—v. 31. Fellow-servants saw the forgiven man being unforgiving. a poor example of the master's kindness. (See I Tim. 4:12.)

B. Shame—vv. 32–34. He is called a "wicked servant" by the master.

1. The master had shown compassion and forgiveness; the servant did not deal in like manner with his fellow-servant.

2. The wicked servant was punished because of his unforgiving spirit and lack of appreciation.

C. Salvation—v. 35. If we forgive, God will forgive us. Note the Lord's Prayer—Matt. 6:12.

Paul gives us good advice in Galatians 6:1–2. (1) If a person fails God, you should forgive and restore him. You, too, may fail. (2) Bear each other's burdens. A Christian's love for God can be measured by the way he treats his fellowmen. A lack of kindness and mercy shows a lack of God in the life.

16

THE SHUT DOOR
Luke 13:24-30

This parable speaks of opportunities that come our way today but are gone tomorrow. Jesus warns that some day the door to heaven will be shut. In Noah's time (Gen. 6:3), God gave men opportunity to be saved, but they rejected it. Now is the day of salvation—II Cor. 6:2. We have no guarantee of what tomorrow will bring—Prov. 27:1. The prophets exhort us to seek the Lord while He may be found—Isa. 55:6. Today may be your last opportunity.

I. **The Way—v. 24**
   Note the words of Jesus in Matt. 7:13-14.
   A. The promise—John 14:1-3. God is preparing a place for us. Note the words of John 3:16, "Not perish, but have everlasting life."
   B. The pathway—John 14:6. Jesus is the only way. There is a way that seems right, but the end is death—Prov. 14:12. Note also Acts 4:12.
   C. The people—those who have their names in the Lamb's book of life—Rev. 20:15. Our names are written in this book when we are born again—John 3:1-8.

II. **The Wrong—vv. 25-26**
   These people were religious but not righteous. Religion is man's way; righteousness is God's way.
   A. Formality without faith—Matt. 7:21-23. One may have all the forms of Christianity, yet not be a child of God. See Eph. 2:8-9.
   B. Ritual without reality—Mark 7:6. Too many give only lip service to the Lord—Luke 6:46. The apostle Paul knew the Lord in a personal way—II Tim. 1:12. To be in Christ is to know Him personally.
   C. Religion without righteousness—Titus 1:16. Their works prove they are not God's children. When one is born again, he becomes a new person—II Cor. 5:17.

III. **The Weeping—vv. 27-28**
   A. The separation from God—v. 27.
      1. Wicked separated from the just—Matt. 13:49.
      2. Sheep separated from the goats—Matt. 25:32.

3. Christian separated from the sinner—Luke 17:34.
B. The sorrow—v. 28.
1. Reality of hell—Ps. 9:17; Dan. 12:2; Matt. 25:41.
2. Residents of hell—Rev. 21:8.
3. Redemption from hell—II Peter 3:9; Rom. 6:23.

The door to heaven is now open. It may be closed tomorrow. Those who hear God's voice but harden their hearts will be destroyed—Prov. 29:1. Don't depend on a religious experience—accept Christ as your personal Saviour today. He will make you righteous with His righteousness. Being religious is not enough—you must be born again.

17

THE TWO SONS
Matthew 21:28–32

I. The Story—vv. 28–30

A. Orders—v. 28. The father of two sons ordered one to work in the vineyard. God calls us to be His sons—(John 1:12; cf. John 15:16; Mark 16:15). God has no hands but our hands. He works through us.

B. Opposition—v. 29. At first the son disobeyed. (See Exod. 20:12; Eph. 6:1–3.) Later this son changed his mind and went to work in the vineyard. When we see we are wrong and repent, God is pleased.

C. Obedience and opposition—v. 30. The second son said he would work, then changed his mind and did not. Isaiah spoke of people loving God with their lips only—Isa. 29:13; see also John 14:15.

II. The Sincerity—v. 31

A. Obedient son—v. 31a. Perhaps the son saw his mistake, then changed his mind. Two of the hardest words for anyone to say are: (1) I'm wrong and (2) I'm sorry. Many do not accept Christ because it is too hard for them to admit they are sinners.

B. Obedient sinners—v. 31b. The publicans (tax collectors) and harlots are closer to receiving the heavenly reward than are the self-righteous Pharisees, who paid tithes, prayed, and fasted (Luke 18:11–12) but whose hearts were far from God. Jesus received more opposition from the religious world than from the secular world.

III. The Salvation—v. 32
Publicans and harlots accepted Christ, while the religious Pharisees rejected Him. Why does man today reject Jesus? Why has man ever rejected him?
A. Refusing to accept the need of a Saviour (Rom. 3:10, 23).
B. Refusing to accept the fact that all men have gone astray (Isa. 53:6).
C. Satan has blinded man to the truth (II Cor. 4:4). Note that Satan is man's father (John 8:44).

Acceptance or rejection—what will be your choice? What will be your choice regarding salvation? Will you accept the Saviour? What will be your choice about practicing the teachings of Christ?—about having daily devotions faithfully?—about full surrender and dedication? Daily choices determine your destiny. It is a personal matter between you and God.

18

THE UNJUST STEWARD
Luke 16:1–13

The sin most likely to be linked with pride is greed. Man isn't satisfied with his possessions but lusts for greater things. The love of money is the root of all evil—I Tim. 6:10.

I. Failure Condemned—vv. 1–3
A. Unjust steward—v. 1. The steward became careless. As Christians, we are stewards (or caretakers) of what God gives us. We are responsible to God for these things.
1. Time—Ps. 90:12. Use your time wisely!
2. Talent—Eccles. 9:10. Use whatever talent you have!
3. Tithes—Mal. 3:8–10. Our tithe belongs to God!
4. Traits—Gal. 5:22–23. Produce the fruit of the Spirit in daily living.

B. Undependable Steward—vv. 2-3. The steward didn't take good care of the master's goods. He didn't expect the master to return so soon. Christ's coming will be soon (Matt. 24:44). These things will soon take place: a) Death—Heb. 9:27, b) Christ's coming—John 14:1-3, c) Judgment—Rev. 20:11-15.

II. Foresight Commended—vv. 4-9
A. Steward's foresight—vv. 4-8. He used his master's money to pay off poor people's debts. The master praised him for his shrewdness. We are not to use God's money for selfish purposes.
B. Sound foresight—vv. 8-9. We should use God's money to advance the kingdom of God. "Bring money into the storehouse" (Mal. 3:10; cf. I Cor. 16:2). Many spend lavishly for their temporal needs but invest little toward their eternal welfare.

III. Faithfulness Counseled—vv. 10-13
A. In service—v. 10. Learn faithfulness in small things. Note the importance of being faithful—Rev. 2:10; Matt. 24:13.
B. In substance—vv. 12-13. God wants our tithes and offerings. We pay over 15 percent in taxes. Is 10 percent too much for God? The government forces us to pay taxes. Love for God will cause us to give Him a tithe.
C. In serving—v. 13. We cannot serve both the world and God. See Matt. 6:33; Prov. 3:5-6.

The teachings of Christ were not popular. Today those who teach His Word will likewise not be popular. Those who love their possessions more than God will show a lack of: (1) self-denial, (2) self-discipline, and (3) self-dedication. Keep your eyes fixed on Christ, and worldly possessions will lose importance.

19

THE WICKED HUSBANDMEN
Matthew 21:33-46

This parable speaks of the rejection of Christ. As the people in the vineyard rejected the servants and the son of the owner, so people reject God's Son and His ministers.

I. **The Story—vv. 33–41**
   A. Parable—v. 33. A vineyard was planted and all preparations provided for its harvesting, including caretakers.
   B. Preparation—v. 34. The owner sent his servants to collect the fruit of the vineyard.
   C. Persecution—vv. 35–39. The servants were killed. The owner (householder) finally sent his son, thinking they would respect him. They killed him!
   D. Plan—vv. 40–41. The householder will destroy wicked men and place responsible husbandmen in control of the vineyard.

II. **The Saviour—vv. 42–44**
   A. Saviour—v. 42. This is a prophecy of Psalm 118:22. Christ is the cornerstone; we are the small stones making up the building.
   B. Sharing—v. 43. "What I mean is that the Kingdom of God shall be taken away from you and given to a nation that will give God his share of the crop" (LB). See John 15:4.
   C. Salvation—v. 44. Those who acknowledge Christ, bowing before Him, will be saved (Phil. 2:10–11). Those who reject the Son of God will be lost.

III. **The Showing—vv. 45–46**
   A. Comparison—v. 45. The chief priests and Pharisees knew Jesus was speaking to them. God's Word speaks to man today. Note: "For whatever God says to us is full of living power: it is sharper than the sharpest dagger, cutting swift and deep into our innermost thoughts and desires with all their parts, exposing us for what we really are"—Heb. 4:12 (LB). See also Rom. 1:16, Eph. 6:17.
   B. Concern—v. 46. They wanted to destroy Christ, but were fearful of the people.

Jesus came to His own people, and they rejected Him—John 1:12a. But those who accepted Him became sons of God—John 1:12b. Whether or not a person believes in God, He will some day be accountable to God. Read Rev. 20:11–15. This judgment will be for those who have rejected Christ. Reject God's Son as the workers in the vineyard rejected the son of the owner and God's judgment will fall on you. Accept Him and you will escape this judgment—John 5:24.

20

THE FOOLISH RICH MAN
Luke 12:15-21

Some measure success by a person's possessions. To God, success is the treasure we have in heaven—Matt. 6:19-21. As Christians, our minds should be on spiritual things—Col. 3:1-2. Earthly possessions will pass away, but our heavenly treasure will endure forever.

I. **The False Riches—v. 15**
   A. Warning—v. 15a. Beware of coveting, which is breaking the tenth commandment—Exod. 20:17. We should not covet our neighbor's house, wife, servants, animals, or anything he has!
   B. Wrong—v. 15b. A man's success or worth is not in earthly possessions. True riches are in Christ. Paul says we brought nothing into this world, and we will take nothing with us when we leave—I Tim. 6:7. Note the folly of self-satisfaction—Rev. 3:17.

II. **The Foolish Reasoning—vv. 16-19**
   A. Success—v. 16. He had good crops. He should be commended for his foresight and plans. As Christians, we should plan for the future with diligence—Eccles. 9:10; Rom. 12:11.
   B. Substance—v. 17. He had more crop success than he could use. Nothing is said of helping or giving to the poor; all was for self. See I John 3:17.
   C. Selfishness—v. 18. He would replace the small barns with larger barns. He didn't seek God's will in this matter. See James 4:15.
   D. Satisfaction—v. 19. He would take his ease and enjoy life. He had all he needed. Note the futility of gaining the world but losing your soul—Mark 8:36.

III. **The Final Results—vv. 20-21**
   A. Death—v. 20. God called this man a fool! "He that trusteth in his own heart is a fool"—Prov. 28:26; also, "Fools make a mock at sin"—Prov. 14:9. He was not preparing for death, which would come that night. Death will come to us (Heb. 9:27) at any time—Prov. 27:1.
   B. Deception—v. 21. "Yes, every man is a fool who gets rich on earth but not in heaven"—LB. Riches may buy an earthly home, but not a heavenly home.

Love for riches often comes between a person and God. A person's home, job, car, or money will often cause him to backslide. Jesus tells us (Matt. 6:25-34) not to be too concerned with our food, homes, and possessions; if we worry about these, we are like the non-Christian. Put Him first in our lives and all these things will be added unto us—Matt. 6:33.

21

THE UNFAITHFUL STEWARD
Luke 12:34-40

God has made us stewards or caretakers of the talents and possessions He has given us. He requires faithfulness—I Cor. 4:2. In this parable, the master has gone away (cf. Acts 1:9-11). The servants are to await his return. As Christians, we await our Lord's return. Prophecies of both Old and New Testaments are being fulfilled. Christ will return soon.

I. **Ready for the Master—vv. 35-36**
   A. Attitude—v. 35. "Be prepared—all dressed and ready"—LB. Christ could return at any time—Matt. 24:44.
   B. Acceptance—v. 36
      1. Foolishness—Luke 21:34. Three things that keep people from being ready: eating, drinking, cares of this life.
      2. Faithlessness—Luke 18:8. When Christ comes, will there be any faith on earth? (Cf. Heb. 11:6).

II. **Return of the Master—v. 37**
   A. Preparation—v. 37. Note: "Find watching."
      1. Sobriety admonished—I Thess. 5:6. Be alert, awake!
      2. Suddenness forewarned—Matt. 25:18. We know not the day nor hour.
   B. Pleasure—v. 38. Be ready to join in the great marriage supper of the Lamb—Rev. 22:1-14. The church (all born-again Christians) will be the bride of Christ.

III. **Rejoicing with the Master—v. 38**
   A. Reality of His coming—v. 38a. "He may come at nine o'clock at

34

night—or even at midnight''—LB. He will come again—John
14:1-3; Matt. 24:40-41.
B. Rejoicing at His coming—v. 38b. ''But whenever He comes there
will be joy for his servants who are ready''—LB. See Rev. 21:4:
no more death, sorrow, crying, nor pain.

IV. **Return of the Master—vv. 39-40**
   A. Unpredictable—v. 39. Not knowing when the thief might strike
   caused the householder to be unprepared. ''But of that day and
   hour knoweth no man, no not the angels of heaven, but my Father
   only''—Matt. 24:36. Note also the comparison of Noah and the
   flood—Matt. 24:37-39.
   B. Unexpected—v. 40. The Master will come at an unexpected hour
   (cf. Acts 1:6-7). His coming will take place in a twinkling of an
   eye—I Cor. 15:52.

Are you a faithful servant? We are told to ''occupy till He comes''—
Luke 19:13. Though watching for His coming, we are to be busy living the
Christian life and seeking to win the non-Christian. His coming will be
unexpected; it will be as the lightning—Matt. 24:27.

22
FAITHFUL AND EVIL SERVANTS
Matthew 24:42-51

In this parable we learn about the coming of Christ. He will come as He
promised in John 14:1-3. There are over 300 references in the New Testament about His return to earth. There are only 70 references about repentance, 19 about water baptism, 6 about communion. One verse out of every
25 in the New Testament has something to say about the coming of Christ.
The prophecies of Matthew 24 have been or are in the process of being
fulfilled. He could come at any time.

I. **Prepared for His Return—vv. 42-44**
   A. Watching—v. 42. As Christians, we are not like those in spiritual

darkness—I Thess. 5:5. We should watch—keep our eyes upon Christ.

   B. Working—v. 43. As one protects his house from a thief, so we must protect our lives from Satan.

      1. Protection—I John 4:4. Greater is God, who is in us, than Satan, who is in the world.

      2. Power—Rom. 8:31. If God be for us, it really doesn't matter who is against us.

   C. Waiting—v. 44. Be ready and waiting. The new birth prepares us for heaven—John 3:1–8. A clean and holy life must follow the new birth—II Cor. 7:1; I John 2:15–17.

II. Promise of His Return—vv. 45–47

   A. Responsibility—v. 45. The servant was responsible to the master. We are responsible to Christ's command—Mark 16:15; John 15:16. His work depends on our response.

   B. Rejoicing—v. 46. Joy at Christ's return will depend on whether or not we are doing His will. David sought God's will—Ps. 143:10. Paul tells us to seek God's will through surrender—Rom. 12:1–2. Note Paul's personal words of surrender—Acts 9:6. Those who do God's will live forever—I John 2:17.

   C. Reward—v. 47. He will reward us. See Rev. 22:12. God keeps a good record book of our deeds—Mal. 3:16.

III. Punishment at His Return—vv. 48–51

   A. Slothful—v. 48. The thinking of the servant that the master would delay his return also pertains to the coming of Christ. See II Peter 3:3–4. People didn't accept the preaching of Noah. It will be the same before Jesus returns.

   B. Sinning—v. 49. While waiting for his lord to come, the servant could become unfaithful, using his waiting time in riotous living, as did the Israelites when Moses was on Mount Sinai for 40 days—Exod. 32:4–28.

   C. Separation—vv. 50–51. The master would return at an unexpected hour. Christ, too, will return at an unexpected time—Acts 1:6–7; Matt. 24:44.

Many will not be ready when Jesus returns. The story He told in Matt. 7:21–23 explains our need to be constantly watching for the return of the Master. It is easy to take our eyes away from Christ in our daily involvements. Be ready, for His coming (as explained by Paul in I Thessalonians 4:13–18) could happen at any time!

23

THE PHARISEE AND THE PUBLICAN
Luke 18:10–14

Jesus here depicts the Pharisee in his "form of godliness"; his pride in his own qualities, his good moral character. In contrast stood the publican, admitting in humility his sin before God. All men are sinners—Rom. 3:10; Jer. 17:9. Good works alone will not make us right with God. We must be born again—John 3:18; II Cor. 5:17.

I. People in the Parable—v. 10
   A. Self-righteous person. "Two men went to the temple to pray. One was a proud, self-righteous Pharisee"—v. 10a (LB). Jesus said our righteousness should exceed that of the Pharisees—Matt. 5:20.
   B. Sinful person—"And the other a cheating tax collector"—v. 10b (LB). This man was a sinner by birth—Rom. 3:23. Though born sinners, we need not remain so.

II. Pharisee's Public Prayer—vv. 11–12
   A. Comparing his person—v. 11a. It is wrong to compare our own spiritual life with others—Matt. 7:1-5.
   B. Comparing his practices—v. 11b.
      1. Not an extortioner. He was honest in money matters.
      2. Not unjust. He was fair in all his dealings.
      3. Not an adulterer. He was morally straight.
      4. He fasted two days a week.
      5. He paid tithes on all his money.
   Our prayer, fasting, and giving should be known only to God. See Matt. 6:1-8, 16-18.

III. Publican's Public Prayer—v. 13
   A. Humility—v. 13a. He was so convinced of his sin, he couldn't even look toward God in heaven. God is near to the humble—Ps. 34:18.
   B. Hopeless—v. 13b. He was sorry for his sin, repentant. Compare David's confession: "I have sinned" (II Sam. 12:13). No excuses were made; he admitted his sin. See also Ps. 51:10.

IV. Pardon Through Prayer

A. Pardon—v. 14a. The publican was forgiven, having confessed his sin. (See I John 1:9; Rom. 10:13).
B. Pride seeks no pardon—v. 14b. God humbles the proud (Prov. 29:23). The Pharisee was abased while the publican was lifted up.

Self-righteousness is sin. We are not saved by good works—Eph. 2:8-9. Titus 3:5 reads, "Not by works of righteousness which we have done, but according to his mercy he saved us, by the washing of regeneration and renewing of the Holy Ghost." Only God can make us righteous. As the publican came to God, he was nothing. So, too, must we come to Him to be clothed in His righteousness.

24

THE LOST SHEEP
Luke 15:1-7

The shepherd of this parable is more concerned with the one lost sheep than the ninety-nine that were safe. This speaks of evangelism—reaching and winning the lost to Christ, perhaps the most needed activity in the church. Too many Christians have little concern for the unreached and unsaved. See Mark 16:15.

I. The Complaint to Christ—vv. 1-2
   A. Curiosity—v. 1. All types of people came to hear Jesus teach. Many were curious, others had special needs. Christ came to seek and save the lost (Matt. 18:11); He came not to condemn, but to convert.
   B. Complaint—v. 2. Self-righteous scribes and Pharisees complained that Jesus ate with sinners. Jesus cleanses from all sin. Note:
      1. God loves all people—John 3:16.
      2. Jesus died for all people—II Peter 3:9.
      3. God forgives all sin—I John 1:7, 9.

II. The Comparison by Christ—vv. 3-6
   A. Parable—vv. 3-4. Who, having one hundred sheep and losing one, would not leave the ninety-nine to seek the one lost sheep? "For God sent not his Son into the world to condemn the world; but that the world through him might be saved"—John 3:17.

B. Protection—v. 5. See the compassion of Jesus (Matt. 9:36).
C. Pleasure through saving—v. 6. The shepherd rejoices when the lost sheep is found. We too rejoice as people accept Christ. Those who sow in tears will reap in joy—Ps. 126:5.(See also John 4:36.)

III. The Conversion to Christ—v. 7
There is rejoicing in heaven when a person accepts Christ. We as Christians also rejoice.
A. God's pardon. The new birth (John 3:1–8) changes man's life. He is a new person in Christ—II Cor. 5:17.
B. God's provision. Isaiah tells of Christ's suffering for man's sin—Isa. 53:5-6. (See also Matt. 27.)
C. God's plan. Christ is the way to heaven—John 14:6. There is no other way—Acts 4:12.
D. God's power. His power cleanses from all sin—Heb. 7:25.

As we draw near to God, we will have compassion for the lost. We will be more faithful in witnessing and seeking to win the lost to Christ.

25

LABORERS IN THE VINEYARD
Matthew 20:1–16

This parable speaks of justice versus faith. At times things happen in our lives that seem unjust. But God allows this for a reason—He is working for our good (Rom. 8:28). Don't worry about justice; God is always fair.

I. The Workers in This Parable—vv. 1–7
A. The natural truth. Five times the man went to get workers for his farm or vineyard—6:00 A.M., 9:00 A.M., 12:00 noon, 3:00 P.M., and 5:00 P.M. The Living Bible says he promised to pay them each $20.
B. The spiritual truth. God needs workers in His vineyard.
   1. Reason for working
      a) The call—John 15:16. God, Himself, is calling us to work for Him.
      b) The command—Mark 16:15. Jesus' last sermon.
      c) The commission—Luke 14:23. Don't give up.
      d) The compassion—Matt. 9:36; Exod. 32:32.

2. Rejection of working. Why people reject God's call and refuse to witness:
    a) Lack of vision—Prov. 29:18; II Cor. 4:4.
    b) Lack of victory—living a defeated life.
    c) Lack of virtue—not bearing the fruit of God's Spirit (Gal. 5:22-23).

II. The Problem in This Parable—vv. 8–12
  A. The compensation—vv. 8-9. Everyone was paid. Christians will be rewarded by God's standards (I Cor. 3:8; II Cor. 9:6; Matt. 6:20-21).
  B. The complaint—vv. 10-12. Those working the whole day received the same as those working part time. They agreed to these wages (see Matt. 16:27; II Cor. 5:10; Rev. 22:17).

III. The Wages in This Parable—vv. 13–16
  A. Promise—v. 13. They agreed to a certain wage—v. 2. What other people are paid is not our concern.
  B. Pay—v. 14. He paid what he had promised. God will be just to: (a) the sinner—Rev. 20:11-15, (b) the Christian—II Cor. 5:10.
  C. Power—v. 15. The owner could do with his money what he wanted. God's way is different than ours—Isa. 55:8.
  D. Promise—v. 16. We could translate this verse to mean, "Those who are forgotten on earth will be rewarded in heaven."

Let God do the judging and rewarding. He knows better than we. He will be fair and just. The Christian has no reason to complain at his treatment. Did Jesus complain? Did Paul—or the other disciples? They suffered much, but they accepted God's will. Complaining is the first step in backsliding. Complaining about what comes into your life is questioning God's will for you.

26

THE SOWER AND SEED
Luke 8:5–15

Jesus used the sower, the seed, and the soil to teach about mankind's reception of God's Word. There are many who hear God's Word, but very few live it. Some accept it for a short time, only to allow sin and self to choke out the Word.

I. The Sower and the Soil—vv. 5-8
A. The sower—v. 5a. A sower went forth to sow his seed.
B. The soil— vv. 5b-8. Note four types of soil:
   1. Wayside—v. 5b. It was a hardened path where the seed could not grow. Birds ate the seed.
   2. Rocky ground—v. 6. With a small amount of soil, it grew quickly and died.
   3. Among thorns—v. 17. It grew, but thorns choked it.
   4. Good ground—v. 8a. It grew and increased.

C. The symbol—v. 8b. "When Jesus had finished saying this, He cried out, 'You have ears, then listen' "—NLT.

II. The Saviour and the Story—vv. 9-10
A. Interest—v. 9. His disciples asked the meaning of this parable.
B. Interpretation—v. 10a. "God has granted you to know the meaning of these parables, for they tell a great deal about the kingdom of God"—LB. God wants us to understand His Word.
C. Ignorance—v. 10b. "But these crowds hear the words and do not understand, just as the ancient prophets predicted"—LB. See II Cor. 4:14; II Tim. 3:7.
Paul speaks of people not seeking God—Rom. 3:11; also of people having their understanding darkened—Eph. 4:18.

III. The Story and the Symbols—vv. 11-15
A. Seed—v. 11. God's Word—It produces faith—Rom. 10:17. God's Word cleanses from sin—Ps. 119:9.
B. Wayside—v. 12. These hear His Word, but Satan steals it away. See I Peter 5:8.
C. Rock—v. 13. They receive the Word, but have no root. Temptation and sin steal it away. Col. 2:7; Matt. 7:24.
D. Thorns—v. 14. Thorns choke out the good seed: (1) Cares— I Peter 5:7 (2) Riches—I Tim. 6:10 (3) Pleasure—Matt. 6:33.
E. Good ground—v. 15. Some hear God's Word and keep it. See Josh. 1:8. Note: "Bring forth fruit with patience."

God wants all Christians to be like the seed falling upon the good ground. His Word will: (1) stablish us—I Peter 3:15, (2) instruct us—II Tim. 2:15, (3) cleanse us—Ps. 119:9, (4) keep us from sin—Ps. 119:11.

Allow His Word to grow within you, to be an active part of your daily life—James 1:22.

27

THE WHEAT AND TARES
Matthew 13:23-30, 37-43

This parable speaks of the separation of the Christian (wheat) and the sinner (tares). God will reward those who love Him with eternal life. Those who reject Him will be eternally doomed. God knows the heart of man and will judge accordingly.

I. **The Sowing of Tares—vv. 24-27**
   A. The parable—vv. 24-25. A man sowed good seed. While he slept, an enemy sowed tares, or weeds (thistles–LB).
   B. The problem—vv. 26-27. The good seed grew among the tares.

II. **The Separating of Tares—vv. 28-30**
   A. Sowing—v. 28. The enemy sowed the tares among the good seed.
   B. Showing—v. 29. The tares are not to be removed, but allowed to grow with the good seed. God will know the Christian from the sinner—II Cor. 5:17; John 8:44.
   C. Separation—v. 30. At harvest time, the wheat will be gathered and the tares will be burned. The Bible speaks also of separating the sheep from the goats—Matt. 25:32, and the wicked from the just—Matt. 13:49. We must die, then comes the judgment—Heb. 9:27.

III. **The Symbols and Tares—vv. 37-39**
   A. Sower—v. 37. The sower of the good seed is Christ.
   B. Seed—v. 38. The field is the world; the good seed are the children of the kingdom—John 1:12; the tares are the children of Satan—John 8:44.
   C. Satan—v. 39. The enemy—Gen. 3:4; Matt. 4:1. The harvest will be at the end of the world (or this age)—Rev. 20:11-15. The reapers are angels—Mark 13:27.

IV. **The Separation of Tares—vv. 40-43**
   A. Separation—v. 40. At judgment, the tares will be put into the fire and burned (Rev. 21:8).

B. Sorrow—v. 41. The tares will be separated from the wheat forever (Rev. 20:10).
C. Suffering—v. 42. Weeping and gnashing of teeth describe feelings of extreme anguish.
D. Saints—v. 43. Christians will shine with God in heaven, having eternal life and joy.

Though the Bible says we will know people by their fruits (Matt. 7:16, 20), we are not to judge others. We make mistakes. "So what right do you have to judge or criticize?"—James 4:12, LB. Finally, God will judge, and His judgment will be right.

28

THE MUSTARD SEED
Matthew 17:19–21

The power of prayer and fasting is shown in this parable. Both are important to the Christian and are tools given to us by God to promote our relationship with Him and to conquer sin.

I. Powerless People—v. 19
A. The disciples wondered why they couldn't cast out the demons as Jesus had instructed.
B. Spiritual weakness—vv. 14–18. The disciples could not cast the demon out of the man's son (John 15:5).
Perhaps Christ used this as a lesson to show the disciples how helpless and weak they were without God's help and the lack of His power in their lives.

II. Practice of Prayer—v. 20
A. Problem—"And Jesus said unto them, because of your unbelief . . ."
1. Heb. 11:6. Without faith, we cannot please God.
2. John 12:37. Jesus performed many miracles, yet people did not believe.
3. Heb. 3:12. "An evil heart of unbelief" leads one away from God.
B. Picture—"Have faith the size of a mustard seed"—a very small

seed that grows to become a tree. This faith would move mountains, do the impossible, perform miracles.
1. Possibility of faith—Matt. 26:26. With God, all things are possible.
2. Power of faith—Mark 9:23. All things are possible if we believe.
3. Practice of faith—James 1:6. Ask in faith; do not waver.

III. The Power of Prayer—v. 21
  A. Purpose of fasting: to weaken Satan's powers—Isa. 58:6; to receive answer to prayer—Isa. 58:8-10.
  B. Power of fasting: Paul—II Cor. 11:27; Jonah (the whole city was converted)—Jonah 3:3-10. All are encouraged to fast—I Cor. 7:5.
  C. Plan of fasting: Daniel—Dan. 9:3; Samuel—I Sam. 7:6; Moses—Deut. 9:18.
  D. People who fasted: Paul—Acts 9:9; Moses—Exod. 34:28; sailors with Paul—Acts 27:33; Elijah—I Kings 19:8; Anna—Luke 2:37; Cornelius—Acts 10:30.

29

THE LEAVEN
Matthew 16:6–12

This parable warns of the false teachings of the Pharisees and Sadducees. Both groups were religious, but their hearts were far from God. Since they were not spiritually minded, they didn't understand the spiritual teachings of Christ.

I. Warning—v. 6
" 'Watch out,' Jesus warned them; 'beware of the yeast of the Pharisees and Sadducees' "—LB. The leaven (or yeast) here refers to the teachings of these two sects.
  A. Religious Pharisees. They were very self-righteous—Luke 18:10-12. They fasted, prayed, paid tithes, but they did not yield to God.
  B. Rejecting Sadducees. They didn't believe in the resurrection, in angels or spirits—Mark 12:18; Luke 20:27; Acts 23:8. Both

groups had a form of godliness, but denied the power thereof— II Tim. 3:5. All false religions and cults have their own writings and forms of religion. But God wants us to have changed lives.

II. Worry—vv. 7–10
The disciples were concerned about their natural food, not understanding spiritual truths.
  A. Confusion—v. 7. Jesus wasn't speaking about bread, but of spiritual truth. Note the power of truth—John 8:32. Jesus is the truth—John 14:6.
  B. Concern—v. 8. Jesus rebuked them, "Oh ye of little faith."
  C. Clarity—vv. 9-10. Jesus reminded them of two times He had fed the multitudes:
    1. 5,000 fed—Matt. 14:15-21. Twelve baskets remained.
    2. 4,000 fed—Matt. 15:32-39. Seven baskets remained.
  Jesus will meet all your needs—Phil. 4:19; Matt. 6:30.

III. Wrong Interpretation—vv. 11–12
  A. Misunderstanding—v. 11. "Why is it that you do not see that I was not talking to you about bread? I was talking to you about keeping away from the yeast of the proud religious lawkeepers and the religious group of people who believe no one will be raised from the dead"—NLT.
  B. Message—v. 12. The disciples finally understood that Jesus was speaking about the false teaching of the Pharisees and Sadducees (cf. II Peter 1:1-3).

God is interested in every phase of your life. He will meet your physical, spiritual, and material needs. Jesus came to give abundant and enjoyable life—John 10:10. To understand God's provisions and blessings, we must live close to Him and follow His Word. Then we will understand His will and way for our lives.